KEVIN OLSON
Concerto Bravo

Notes from the Publisher

Composers In Focus is a series of original piano collections celebrating the creative artistry of contemporary composers. It is through the work of these composers that the piano teaching repertoire is enlarged and enhanced.

It is my hope that students, teachers, and all others who experience this music will be enriched and inspired.

Frank J. Hackinson, Publisher

Notes from the Composer

The origins of the word "concerto" have long been debated by music historians. Some have maintained that the word derives from the Latin word *concertare*, which means "to fight or contend with". Others believe it comes from *conserere*, meaning "to join or bind together". I believe this concerto falls best in the second category, with the two pianos combining into an exciting, interactive work. Playing concertos requires the soloist to listen carefully and play out when the solo part is the focus, but to blend with the accompanimental part when it isn't. Work to play with rhythmic precision so you're in sync with the second part. And, finally, bring out all the expression markings for an artistic and dramatic interpretation. You may just hear some "bravos" of your own after your fantastic performance!

Best wishes,

Kevin Olson

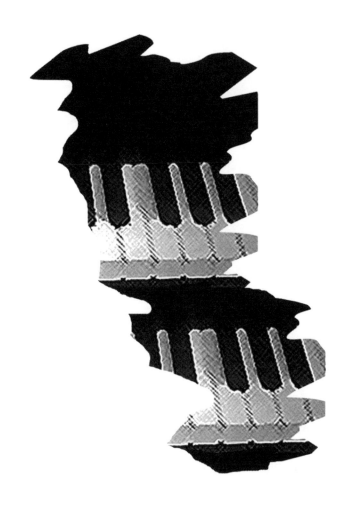

Contents

4

commissioned for the 50th anniversary of the Utah Music Teachers Association
October 2006

Concerto Bravo

I.

Kevin Olson

FF1706

8

10

14

II.

Freely; with expression (♩ = 132)

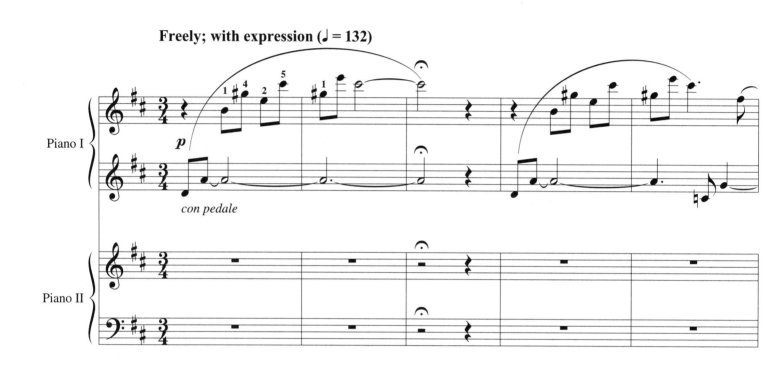

con pedale

16

20

FF1706

III.

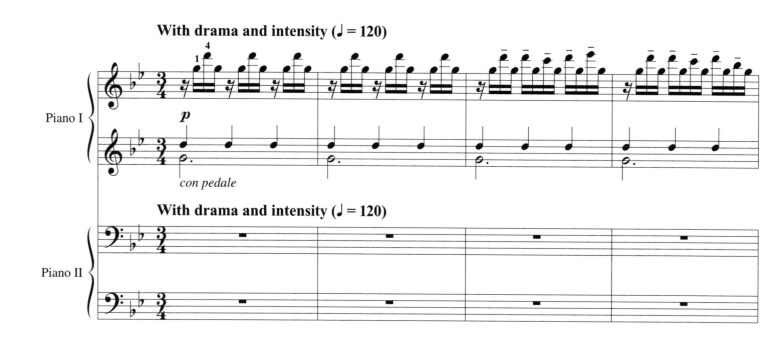

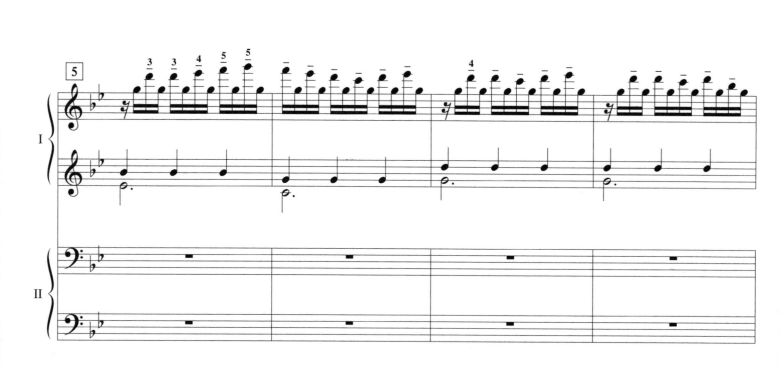

32

FF1706